A Wibble
Called Bipley

(and a few Honks)

Margot Sunderland

Illustrated by
Nicky Armstrong

 Routledge
Taylor & Francis Group

LONDON AND NEW YORK

ONCE THERE WAS a wibble called Bipley. He was a very soft and loveable wibble, as wibbles often are.

Wibbles are also great fun to be with, because they can play well and they laugh a lot, and Bipley could too!

Wibbles are particularly good at
           rolling
                     down
                          grassy
                                    banks,

having giggling parties,

and blowing BIG, BIG bubbles that last for as long as you want them to . . .

. . . and they are also very good at cuddles.

But one day, someone did something which hurt Bipley so badly, that it felt like his heart had broken into little pieces. He felt so much pain that he thought he would never be able to mend.

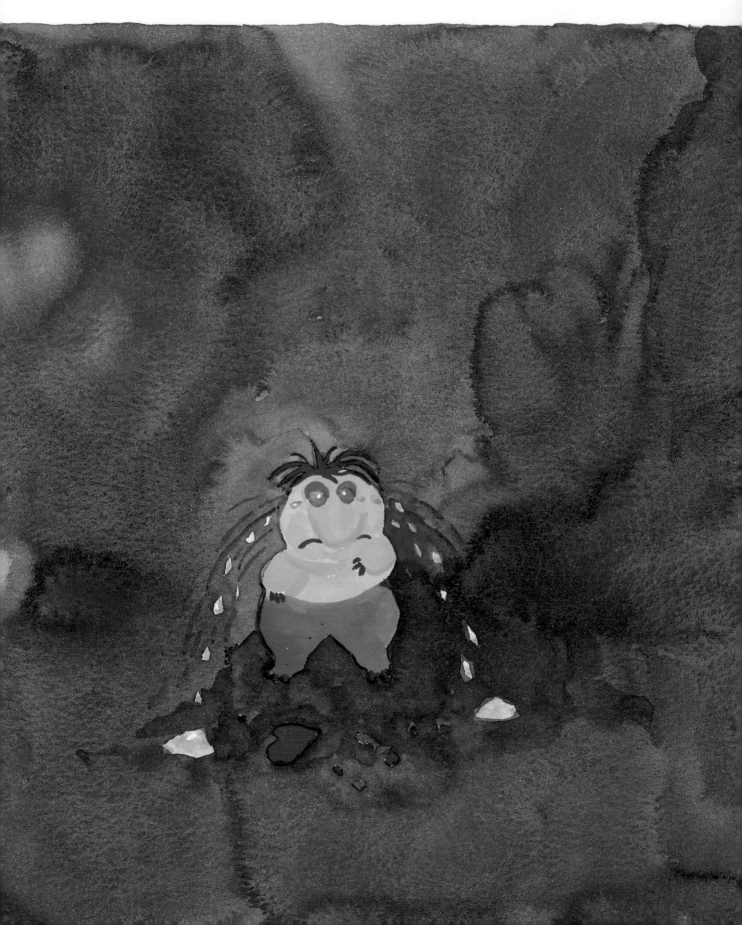

And this meant that Bipley had a very important thought, "It's *because* I'm so soft and gentle that I got so hurt," he said to himself. "If I hadn't loved, if I'd been hard and tough instead, it wouldn't have happened."

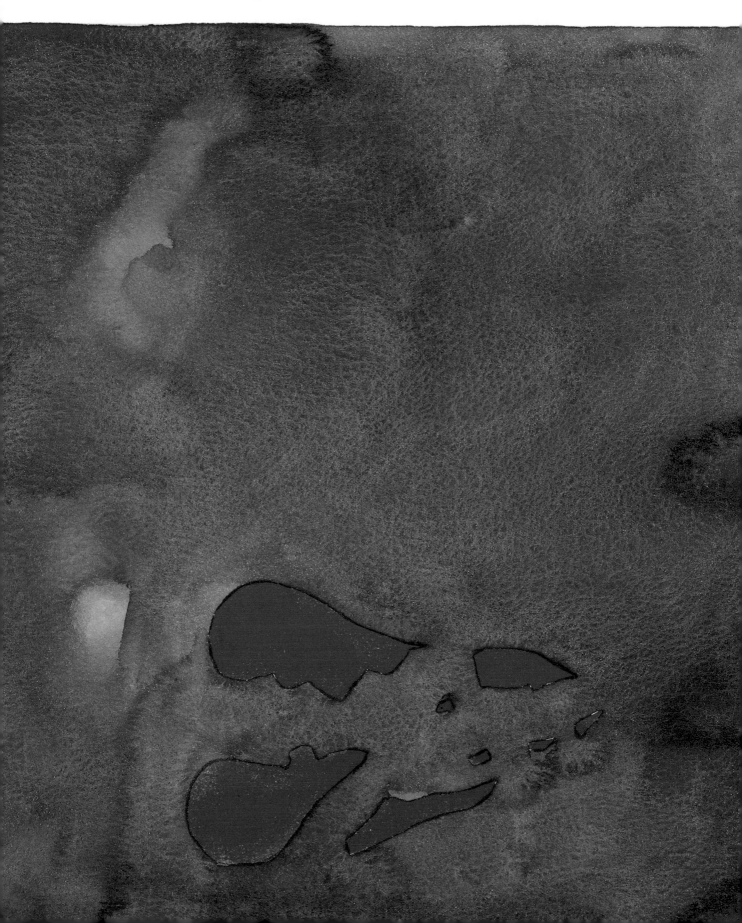

By now Bipley was so full of tears, and so full of the terrible pain from his broken heart, that he decided he must *do* something. ANYTHING! "Ah yes, I'll walk into Wibble Wood," he thought, "and find my favourite place by the lake. Being there always makes me feel good."

Bipley's favourite place in Wibble Wood was a lovely spot for picnicking with super swings, two slides and a great big sand-pit. Bipley thought that if he could just sit on one of the super swings and look at the water's gentle lapping, it might somehow lap right over him and make him feel better, because by now the pain in his heart had got just awful.

Along the way to the super swings, Bipley bumped into three
honks. Honks are big, tough creatures who wear dark glasses,
ginormous overcoats, and biscuit tins for hats. They have
square knees and glossy black toes which glow in the dark.

One of the honks, called Harry Honk, could see from Bipley's face that Bipley had a broken heart. "Look here, old chap," said Harry Honk, "you're silly walking around being so soft and loving. That's *just* how people get hurt. I used to be like you, until I decided enough was enough. I didn't want to get hurt any more. I said to myself, 'Get tough, Harry! Get tough!'"

"So how do you get tough?" asked Bipley who had absolutely no idea. "Well, guess what we have under our ginormous coats?" asked Harry. Bipley guessed all sorts of things, from fizzy pop, to skate boards, to hot dogs, which were all completely wrong.

So the honks undid their coats, and there before Bipley's very eyes were three big walls! "We built these walls to keep our hearts from getting hurt," said one of the honks proudly. "And that means that now we don't feel hurt any more. You've just gotta find a wall too Bipley, so that *your* heart can't get hurt any more either."

Bipley thought this was an excellent idea. So he started to look for something in Wibble Wood. After a lot of searching without finding, Bipley saw a big block of tough stuff lying by a little bush. He picked it up and found a way to fix it to his heart.

As soon as Bipley had done this, he felt very different inside. He didn't feel hurt any more. He didn't feel his tears all piled up inside him. He didn't feel the pain of his broken heart. In fact, Bipley felt tough. And Harry Honk gave Bipley a pair of dark glasses and showed him how to make his knees go square, and how to paint his toes black so that they glowed in the dark.

Then up popped a family of wibbles who were
off to have a picnic in Wibble Wood.

"Wibble off!" shouted Bipley, from behind his dark
glasses and his square knees. And the wibbles were so
frightened that they all ran away.

But two little wibbles were in such a hurry
that they fell over each other
                and rolled
                    into a very muddy puddle!

Bipley laughed at them in their
muddy mess and shouted, "You
stupid little wibblywimps!"

The little wibbles
shivered with fear.

Now Bipley had never felt like this before. And what he felt was POWER, POWER, POWER!

Instead of being the one who got hurt, now *he* could be the one who did the hurting!

It made him feel tall, so tall, and big, so big, big as the biggest tree in the wood. POWER rushed through Bipley's wibbly body, so he tingled with excitement. Gone was his hurt! Gone were his tears! Gone was his broken heart! He was flying! He was on a big dipper at a fairground! He was King of Kings! He was MIGHTY BIPLEY!

And each time more wibbles came to visit the picnic spot in Wibble Wood, Bipley would shout at them, and be even ruder and louder than the time before, until after a while there was no one left picnicking there at all! Not even one little wibble!

But when Bipley had played on the swings seventeen times, and slid down the slides twenty-five times, and made forty-six sandcastles in the sand-pit, he began to feel a bit lonely. His feeling of power had lost some of its fireworky feel.

He tried to to get it back by being horrible to a passing slug, calling it a "SMELLY SLUGGY SUPER-YUK!" but that didn't work either, because the slug was lost in a wonderful dream about a very juicy lettuce which he had slugged over that morning.

And just as Bipley was thinking about squashing the slug,
   it slid away
            into some prickly shrub!

So Bipley sat down, feeling rather flat and dull, just like you do sometimes the day after your birthday, or when there's only a heap of burnt-out squibs, the morning after bonfire night.

Just when Bipley was wondering what to do next, he noticed a little buttercup called Beryl.
(In fact all the buttercups in Wibble Wood are called Beryl. They like it that way.)

Now for some reason Beryl Buttercups are not at all frightened of honks. In fact Bipley's shouting sounded to Beryl like a rather strong wind, and Beryls quite like wind.

So Beryl just smiled at Bipley, and told him how much she liked his square knees and his biscuit tin hat. She said that his sandcastles were the most lovely sandcastles she had ever seen.

She wondered if she might sit on one for a while?

Now usually, when people say nice things to Bipley it gives him a warm glow inside. But this time, he just felt cold. It was then that Bipley knew something awful had happened.

The tough stuff had stopped any hurt coming into his heart, but it had also stopped lovely warm feelings coming in too!

Then Beryl said, "Oh, isn't it beautiful around here! Look at the blue sky and the green, green grass. See how the sun shimmers on the lapping water." Then Bipley felt even worse, because when he looked at the sky, it was all grey. And when he looked at the grass it was grey too. And when he looked at the lake all he saw was a big pool of dirty water. Somehow, ever since Bipley had become a honk, all the warmth and light and colour had gone out of his world.

"I don't see anything beautiful," said Bipley, "all I see is the smelly rubbish bin in the picnic area, and that broken swing over there." Now Beryl was a very wise buttercup. "Oh dear," she said, "I think I know what's happened, Bipley. I think you must have closed your heart. That's what happens when you close your heart. Everything goes grey and dull."

So Bipley sat by the grey lake in Wibble Wood and thought and thought. "If I keep the tough stuff around my heart, I need never feel hurt again. But then having the tough stuff around my heart means that I can't feel any of the beautiful things in the world." Bipley was very, very stuck. It felt like he was sitting next to the biggest problem in his life.

Just at that moment, along came Doris the tortoise and Poggle the hedgehog. Bipley told them about his problem. "Well," said Doris "when I'm with people who are nasty to me, I just go into my shell. But when I'm with nice people I come right back out again." "Well," said Poggle, "if I'm with people who are frightening or cruel, I curl into a ball. But if I'm with my friends I come back out again." Poggle went on, "Bipley, I think maybe your problem is that somehow you've become your wall. So now there's more wall than Bipley."

Bipley listened very carefully and thanked
Doris and Poggle, because he'd just had
a great idea. He tried to take off his wall,
but it was very difficult as it had somehow
stuck to him, rather like a skin. But after a huge amount of
pushing and pulling, it came off. Then Bipley made a new wall
– this time, a POCKET-SIZE ONE! "I'll just bring it out,"
thought Bipley, as he put the little wall in his pocket, "if
someone is being horrible to me." But then something else
happened . . .

Bipley's heart, which had grown hard and closed because it
had been behind the wall of tough stuff for so long, began to
melt. And Bipley felt a new pain rather like what happens
when a part of you which has been very, very cold, starts to
get warm again, and rather like what happens when a
snowman melts and there's a lot of water on the lawn. And
then all Bipley's tears, which had frozen behind the tough
stuff, came flooding out, and Bipley started to cry very loudly.

But this meant that lots of wibbles heard him, and they appeared, as if from nowhere. "It's Bipley!" they said with glee. "Yippee! Bipley's not a honk any more. He's becoming a wibble again!" And Bipley snuggled up to them and cried about how lonely he'd felt as a honk and about how his world had become so horribly grey.

Bipley also told his wibble friends about how he'd felt so big and powerful over little soft frightened creatures, but that somehow that had made him lose everything warm and gentle about himself, and feel awfully, awfully empty. As Bipley snuggled into his wibble friends and told his sad tale, the sky started to become blue again, and Bipley could feel the sun once more. He saw how it shimmered on the beautiful lake.

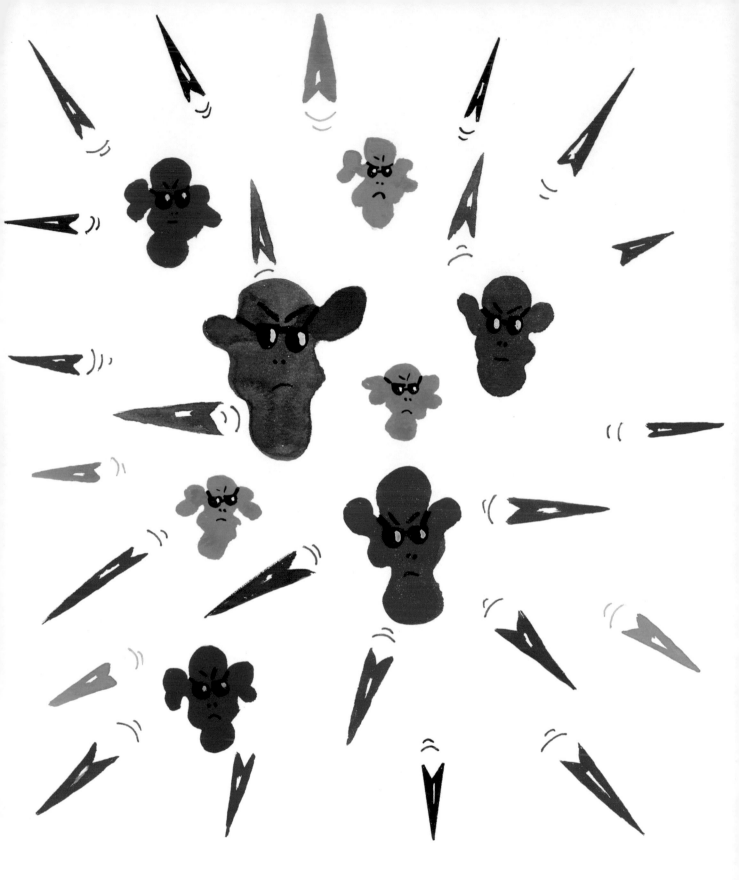

And to this day, Bipley still carries a little wall in his pocket, as do lots and lots of other wibbles now. Bipley's story made them think about how being soft and open to everyone all of the time is not a sensible thing to do at all, because it means that people who want to ZAP you with their bad, spiky feelings can do so far too easily.

So now, if you're ever around when people who feel bad about themselves try to dump their bad, spiky feelings onto a wibble, then you'll see how the wibble will get out his little wall. You'll see how those spiky feelings never get to the wibble. Instead they just fall into a ditch or a puddle, or stick right back on to the spiky person, like some rather smelly glue.

But as for Bipley, he was no fool. Deep down, he knew that if, in the future, someone important to him or someone who he loved very, very much was to hurt him again, then the little wall in his pocket wouldn't be enough to protect him. What should he do? Bipley decided to take a risk. This time he would use his wall when he needed to, but *without* closing his heart as well!

From his time as a honk, he'd learnt that it's easy to get all hard and closed after you've been hurt. But he'd also learnt how grey the world becomes when you do that. Bipley knew now that the bravest thing of all is to keep your heart open, so that you can love someone again . . . when you're ready to, when you want to.

And after that, Bipley ran off happily, to join the latest giggling party with all his wibble friends, and a few honks . . .

. . . friendly ones, of course!